■ "THE CONVERSATION™" is a meeting desi[...]
business owners about transitioning out of their busine[...]

During "The Conversation™" your situation, objectives, and challenges should be discussed in detail. Company performance, retirement goals, transition options and your desire to continuing running the business are all things that should be considered. The purpose is to provide you with a sense of direction and control in the face of the uncertainty and stress generated by every company's inevitable transition.

Are you in need of "The Conversation™"? Here are a few questions you should ask yourself to see if it is time to begin transition planning. *(If you completed this assessment in the book, circle your score below and move to the next exercise.)*

YES   NO

1. It's time to do something different with my life.

2. My burning desire to compete is failing. I may be burned out.

3. My children are no longer interested or capable of running the business.

4. I've been approached by a competitor/the market for companies like ours is hot and so it's a good time to sell.

5. There has been a health scare and it's time to "stop and smell the roses."

6. I really don't know what my business is currently worth.

7. My company is losing market share, revenues and/or profits.

8. In order to diversify my personal assets, I want to take some chips off the table.

9. There are relationship issues within my family or partnership which are making the business emotionally draining.

10. I want to leave my business on my terms from a position of strength.

Results – Based on Total Yes Responses –

0-3 You may not be planning a transition soon, but we can help you create a written exit strategy that will help protect the value of the business you've built.

4-6 You would benefit from "The Conversation™" for planning purposes.

7-8 Your transition is coming soon. "The Conversation™" would be beneficial now.

9-10 "The Conversation™" should have happened years ago.

If your results recommend you have a conversation now or in the near future, we are here to help.

■ TRANSITION TIMELINE

Recognize that exiting your business is a process, not an event. Most business owners start too late. More planning = more options = more value. Plan your exit on your terms.

When do you want to be out of the business? Complete this exercise to uncover when you need to start.

How old are you today? _____

Example

65	−	2 years	−	9 months	−	12 months	=	61
Age "out" of business		Time to prepare company for sale (6 mo - 3 yrs)		Time to sell business (6 - 12 mo)		Time to transition past sale (6 - 12 mo)		Age to start sales process

65	−	1 year	−	9 months	−	5 years	−	6 months	=	57
Majority/ minority recap age "out" of business		Time to prepare company for recap (6 mo - 3 yrs)		Time to sell/recap business (6 - 12 mo)		Time post sale/recap *could be much shorter if proper mgmt team in place (3-7 yrs)		Time to transition past sale (6 - 12 mo)		Age to start recap phase

---

	−		−		−		=	
Age "out" of business		Time to prepare company for sale (6 mo - 3 yrs)		Time to sell business (6 - 12 mo)		Time to transition past sale (6 - 12 mo)		Age to start sales process

	−		−		−		−		=	
Majority/ minority recap age "out" of business		Time to prepare company for recap (6 mo - 3 yrs)		Time to sell/recap business (6 - 12 mo)		Time post sale/recap *could be much shorter if proper mgmt team in place (3-7 yrs)		Time to transition past sale (6 - 12 mo)		Age to start recap phase

Dear Business Owner,

The reason I created this workbook is because too many people (including myself) read a book, get a bunch of good ideas, then put the book down and never implement a one. At the end of the day, that doesn't move the needle forward.

In creating this workbook, my hope is that you'll take the time to complete each exercise as they're set up for you. These tools have been created to help you advance in three important, but often forgotten, areas:

1. Maximize your value drivers. Know how to exit your business on top of your game.
2. Understand what you need to live your next best chapter/ideal lifestyle.
3. Make sure you're psychologically and emotionally ready to transition your company.

I've found that too many people put their business on the market because they're reacting to a trigger – and it's usually not a positive one. In the rush to sell, they miss out on these critical steps that could make their transition easier, more valuable, and more fulfilling.

There are almost endless consultants (private and government backed) who will help you start a business, write a business plan, or create a strategy for growth. But very few help you figure out how best to "finish strong" or sell your business. My goal is to help you with that very important last step of your business journey.

Exiting your business will likely be the largest financial transaction of your life. I want that transition to be something you can be proud of – something that meets your financial needs, ensures your legacy, and sets your employees and your business up for success for many years to come.

But most of all, I want you to exit your business on your terms. I hope you find my book "Finish Strong: Selling Your Business on Your Terms" and this companion workbook are tools to help you get there.

My best to you,

Scott Bushkie, CBI, M&AMI
Founder and Managing Partner
Cornerstone Business Services

CHAPTER 1 - IS IT TIME TO HAVE "THE CONVERSATION™?"

"IT IS NOT HOW YOU START... BUT HOW YOU FINISH. FINISH STRONG!"

CRITICAL QUESTIONS EVERY BUSINESS OWNER SHOULD ASK THEMSELVES

Is the business your largest asset? ___Yes ___No ___Don't Know

What if today was your last day on Earth? What would happen to:

Your business:

Your family:

Your employees:

Your legacy:

1. Do you have enough passive investments that if you shut down your business you would live your ideal lifestyle? ___Yes ___No

2. Do you rely on the business as your primary source of income? ___Yes ___No

3. Do you need to successfully sell your business to live your ideal lifestyle? ___Yes ___No ___Don't Know

4. Do you have a written plan as to how, when, and why you will exit your business? ___Yes ___No   If not, when will you create one? Date:_____

5. Have you had a valuation done in the last 2-3 years by a respected M&A firm that understands the current market for a business like yours? (Not just formula driven valuations) ___Yes ___No

6. Do you have sufficient life insurance to protect you, your family, and the business if something were to happen to you? ___Yes ___No

7. Have you met with your CPA to understand the tax ramifications of a potential sale? ___Yes ___No

8. Have you met with a financial/wealth management advisor to determine what you need to live your ideal lifestyle? ___Yes ___No

If you answered these questions opposite of the ideal key below, don't worry, most owners don't have all the answers. Continue to use this workbook and call Cornerstone to learn how, together, we can help you reach your goals and ideal lifestyle.

Ideal Answers... 1: Yes; 2: No; 3: No; 4: Yes; 5: Yes; 6: Yes; 7: Yes; 8: Yes

■ LIFE WHEEL

Rate your level of satisfaction with each area of your life on a scale of 0 - 10 (0 = lowest level of satisfaction and 10 = highest level of satisfaction). Place a dot on the line that represents your score. Next shade inside the circle for each section, creating a "wheel." How bumpy is the ride?

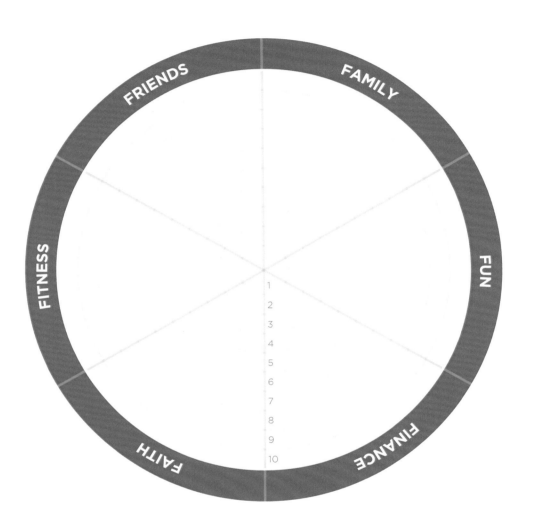

AREA	NOW	GOAL	ACTION ITEMS — HOW WILL YOU IMPROVE THIS AREA?
FRIENDS			
FAMILY			
FUN			
FINANCE			
FAITH			
FITNESS			

▌ WHAT DIFFERENT HATS DO YOU CURRENTLY WEAR?

1

2

3

4

5

6

7

8

9

10

Are there any hats you **do not** want to wear? Why? Can you take them off? If so, who can you transition them to?

▌ WHAT'S MISSING FROM YOUR LIFE RIGHT NOW?

1

2

3

4

5

▌ WHAT THREE THINGS WOULD YOU DO IF YOU KNEW YOU COULD NOT FAIL?

1

2

3

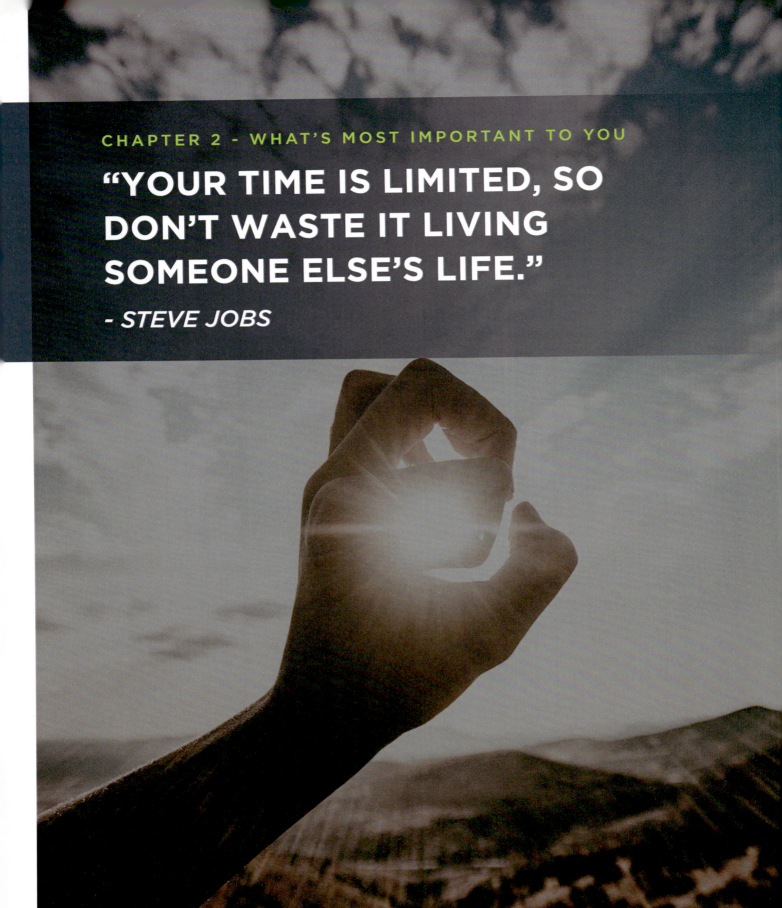

CHAPTER 2 - WHAT'S MOST IMPORTANT TO YOU

"YOUR TIME IS LIMITED, SO DON'T WASTE IT LIVING SOMEONE ELSE'S LIFE."

- STEVE JOBS

▮ VALUES MENU

Your values underpin the choices you make. In this chapter, we're asking you to think about what you want most out of a business transition. Before you make that ranking (next exercise), stop to think about what really matters to you in life. What do you stand for?

Consider this values menu and circle the values that are most integral to who YOU are personally. If a value is missing, add it in the extra space. Circle up to 10 values that you believe best define you. Then star the 3 that rank the highest in your eyes.

Action	Curiosity	Growth	Strength
Adventure	Evolution	Happiness	Success
Ambition	Excellence	Impact	Sustainability
Authenticity	Faith	Ingenuity	Trust
Belonging	Family	Integrity	Vision
Care	Freedom	Loyalty	Well-being
Community	Fun	Passion	
Courage	Generosity	Respect	
Craftsmanship	Gratitude	Responsbility	

If you have a spouse or a business partner, what do you think they value most?

▪ DEAL PRIORITIES—WHAT IS IMPORTANT TO YOU?™

In business transactions, rarely does either side get everything they want in a deal. That is why it is important to understand what you value most. In talking with sellers in the past 2+ decades, we have found that most sellers really don't know what they truly want out of a sale or how they would prioritize different deal points.

By taking the time now to reflect and to better understand what "success" means to you in an exit, you will have the best opportunity to get the key elements you are looking for and leave on your terms. Remember, you only get one chance to do this right!

Please rank each of the following. "1" is the most important and "10" is the least important to you. There are no wrong answers — it is truly what matters to you. Each answer should have its own number, i.e. there should not be two #1s, etc.

This may seem to be a simple survey but many of our sellers told us it was tougher than expected to choose between some of the different deal points. Take the time needed to really think about each point, and discuss it with your spouse and/or partner. Again, no right or wrong answers!

CHAPTER 2

FINISH STRONG - WORKBOOK

VISIBLE
20%

INVISIBLE
80%

VALUE

PROTECT EMPLOYEES

CULTURE FIT

AMOUNT OF TIME
NEEDED FOR
TRANSITION AFTER
THE SALE

DEAL STRUCTURE

LEGACY FACTORS

ETC.

A._____ Highest value overall: This means that you want as much money for your business as possible and all other deal points come second. You do not care as much about any other items including cash at close or structure. You will agree to a more creative structure, many times with a larger portion tied to the growth of the company or future performance.

B._____ Cash at close: You are willing to sacrifice overall consideration and willing to take less if you can get more cash at close. This is typically chosen by a seller who may be burned out or just needs a clean break and does not want to have an on-going relationship with the company or worry about payments being made to them. This may eliminate some buyers desiring a more creative structure.

C._____ Transition time frame/role: The role you want to transition into, and the time in which the buyer wants you to transition, is very important to you. You want to do what you are passionate about without having to worry about day-to-day operations. If you were to receive two offers, you would choose the offer with less money to have the lifestyle you want.

Circle your ideal transition time frame:

- 0-6 months
- 6 months-1 year
- 1 year-3 years
- 3 years-5 years

Circle your ideal role after the sale

- CEO/same position
- Business development
- Inventor/creator of new products/services
- Board of directors
- Other _____

D._____ Protect employees: If this is high on your list, you are considering the future status of your employees and their continued employment with the company after the sale. Again, if you choose this as number "1," you would take a lower offer if it were better for your employees.

E._____ Equity rollover: This allows you to divest shares of your company while retaining some equity. Your remaining shares will increase in value if everything works the way it should. You diversify your personal risk while giving the buyer the opportunity to build the company with their vision, contacts, resources, and capital. Ideally, when the business is sold a second time, your shares will be worth much more than when you sold initially. There is risk, like any contingent payment, that things won't work out, but most buyers are vetted and have successful track records.

F._____ Legacy factor: This means it's very important to you to see your business continue to be successful in future years. It also means the business name will most likely stay the same.

G._____ Closing date: If you are in a hurry to divest yourself of your business, finding a buyer who can close the deal soonest is important.

H._____ Best chance to close: This means choosing a buyer who may not give you the best deal but who will be most likely to close the deal.

I._____ Real estate: Buyer will buy or lease real estate at current location at a fair market value.

Circle what you would like to do with real estate:

Lease

Sale

Keep for other purposes

J._____ Compensation for role: This means it is important for you to get fair market (or above) compensation for your time as an employee or consultant to the company after the sale. This would include health insurance.

CHAPTER 3 - YOU HAVE MORE OPTIONS THAN YOU KNOW

"IF YOU DON'T HAVE THE INFORMATION YOU NEED TO MAKE WISE CHOICES, FIND SOMEONE WHO DOES." - *LORI HILL*

▮ WHAT ARE MY TOP 3 EXIT OPTIONS?

Choose the top 3 ways you think you'd like to exit your business. Common options include:

- Sell 100% of your business
- Sell the majority of your business
- Sell a minority stake
- Sell to family members
- Sell to your management team
- Transfer to employees via an ESOP
- Divest a division
- Close your doors
- Death or disability

1 _____
2 _____
3 _____

▮ CONTROL/LIQUIDITY

If you're looking to diversify your assets, this table indicates different exit or recapitalization options, ranked in order from most owner control, to most liquidity.

MINORITY RECAPITALIZATION	MAJORITY RECAPITALIZATION
Retain ownership control and preserve operational control	Ownership control transfers to new majority owner
Obtain partial liquidity to diversify assets	More cash to owner at close
Benefit from ongoing success in the business via a potential future liquidity event	Less economic participation in future growth of company
Allow family members to remain active in the business	Owners less concerned about the transitioning control to family members and existing management team
Lower debt / leverage levels	Less concern about the future debt / leverage
Potential to regain 100% ownership by buying back equity	Very difficult to regain 100% ownership

■ PRIVATE EQUITY PLAYBOOK

The graphic below demonstrates how private equity firms build value in your company.

■ 10 KEY QUESTIONS TO ASK BEFORE CHOOSING A BUYER

1. Does the buyer proactively provide complete references?

2. Do they do what they say they're going to do?

3. Is the buyer asking the right questions?

4. What is the buyer's track record with similarly-sized companies?

5. What does the potential buyer offer beyond capital?

6. What team will management work with, and is this team empowered to make decisions?

7. If a private equity firm, do they have a committed fund or do they raise money deal by deal? Can the buyer prove the ability to finance the deal?

8. What is the buyer's communication style and expectations after the deal closes?

9. What does the exit transaction look like?

10. Can you see yourself having fun together?

■ WHO IS THE BEST BUYER FOR YOUR BUSINESS?

One of the first steps in the lengthy research process of developing a "target" (buyer) list is to brainstorm with you the owner. Review the different strategies below for acquisition and make a note of different types of buyer groups or specific companies you think would make synergistic/strategic sense to purchase your company.

HORIZONTAL
When a company merges with or acquires another company that provides the same service or product to final customers.

VERTICAL
Similar to horizontal, but the companies are in different stages of production.

CONCENTRIC
When two businesses have the same customers in a specific industry, but they offer different products and services.

CONGLOMERATE
If a merger happens between two completely unique businesses, it is considered a conglomerate.

CHAPTER 4 - TRANSITIONING TO FAMILY OR MANAGEMENT

> "IT IS MUCH MORE DIFFICULT TO KNOW WHAT IS FAIR THAN WHAT IS UNFAIR."
>
> — MICHAEL JOSEPHSON

■ FAMILY MEETING

Your exit impacts a lot of stakeholders, including your spouse and family. We strongly suggest you include your family early in the discussion process. Give them an opportunity to make their interests known and learn the options available.

Initial Below
_____ You
_____ Family/Other

Had meeting with family and/or all decision makers on exit options.

© 2021

The remainder of this chapter may not be applicable if you are not considering an internal transfer

■ CEO SUCCESSOR QUIZ

Selecting a successor is critical to the sustainability of your business. When reviewing your exit options, it's important to define the role of the successor and consider the eligible candidates objectively.

Focus

1. What unique value-added advantages do you personally bring to the business?

2. Who could replace you who could also provide these same unique advantages?

3. What would need to change to make it desirable for you to continue in your role?

4. What would need to change to make it desirable for someone else to take on your role?

Passion

5. What aspect of the business is your pride and joy?

6. Who else shares the same pride and joy for that aspect of the business?

7. After you step aside, what would you like to see happen with the business?

8. Who do you know who would wish to take the business in a different direction?

Dependability

9. What will be the hardest part about leaving this business in the hands of others?

10. Who do you know that appreciates the significance (to you) of that hand-off?

11. Where have you failed to reach your own goals for this business?

12. Who has the capacity and talent to meet those uncompleted goals?

Relationships

13. What is it about your talent mix that made you an ideal fit for running this business?

14. Who do you know who has that same talent mix?

15. Who is your best customer and how did you build a strong relationship with them?

16. Who do you know who could build that kind of relationship with new customers?

Success

17. Where could/should the business be optimized to make it even more successful going forward?

18. Who do you know who could add value in those areas not yet maximized?

19. What persistent problems or challenges have you yet to conquer in this business?

20. Who do you know that has the drive and interest to tackle those challenges?

Reflection

21. Based on your answers to the questions above, as of today, who (if anyone) might be suited to fill your shoes?

22. If you see a potential successor, what reservations do you have that you would like to explore? Does this individual have the necessary time to devote to the business?

23. What would it take to equip this individual to assume your role six months from today?

■ KEY ACCOUNTABILITIES

Objective: Clearly outline the business owner's role and priorities which they will be accountable for to objectively determine if the potential successor has what it takes to be successful in this role.

It's important to know what you're looking for and why. By doing this exercise, you will determine the key accountabilities, skills, and competencies needed for the position.

What are key accountabilities? Key accountabilities are the primary responsibilities of the job. The key accountabilities summary is made up of three to five primary roles for the position.

To get started, we've identified the most common key accountabilities below. Feel free to chose from those or create your own.

Most Common Key Accountabilities for Business Owners

• **Visioning**: Creating a vivid, credible image of an ideal future state for the business while making sure to reinvent the business every 5 years to stay relevant. Adapting proactively is crucial to success.

• **Leadership:** Creating a sense of purpose that is exemplified by a recognized set of behaviors and shared beliefs that shapes the values and standards of the business. Successful business owners know how to engage and work with key stakeholders to make a business impact.

• **External Face:** Strategically position the brand of the business in the market.

• **Strategic Customer Engagement:** Connect with potential customers in new ways across multiple channels.

• **Innovation:** Create IP assets for the business.

• **Sales:** Accountable for building a new sales pipeline, building relationships and providing customers with solutions that result in revenue generation for the business.

• **Strategy and Alignment:** Responsible for translating the vision into a compelling and relevant strategy for the entire business. What business are we in and what business are we not in?

• **Driving for Results:** The ability to reliably produce results is one of the most essential behaviors for business owners.

• **Supplier Relations:** Facilitate and support established and emerging relationships with suppliers.

• **Industry Relations:** Maintain an active presence among trade associations and other business entities.

Ask yourself the following questions:
• What key results reflect superior performance (think 6+ months into the job)?
• What activities, motivations, and competencies are most likely to produce these results?

Does your successor have what it takes? According to research by Aperio Consulting Group, 77% of a business owner's success is due to the human factor. It's crucial to determine if the successor has what it takes to be successful. To take a deeper dive and assess them against the successful owners in the study, please visit: thinkaperio.com/cornerstone.

Example

Key Accountability	Priority	Potential Successor's Rating (Scale of 1-10*)
Visioning	1	_____
Shape the Culture and Values	2	_____
Strategic Customer Engagement	3	_____
Supplier Relations	4	_____
Industry Relations	5	_____

Key Accountability	Priority	Potential Successor's Rating (Scale of 1-10*)
	1	_____
	2	_____
	3	_____
	4	_____
	5	_____

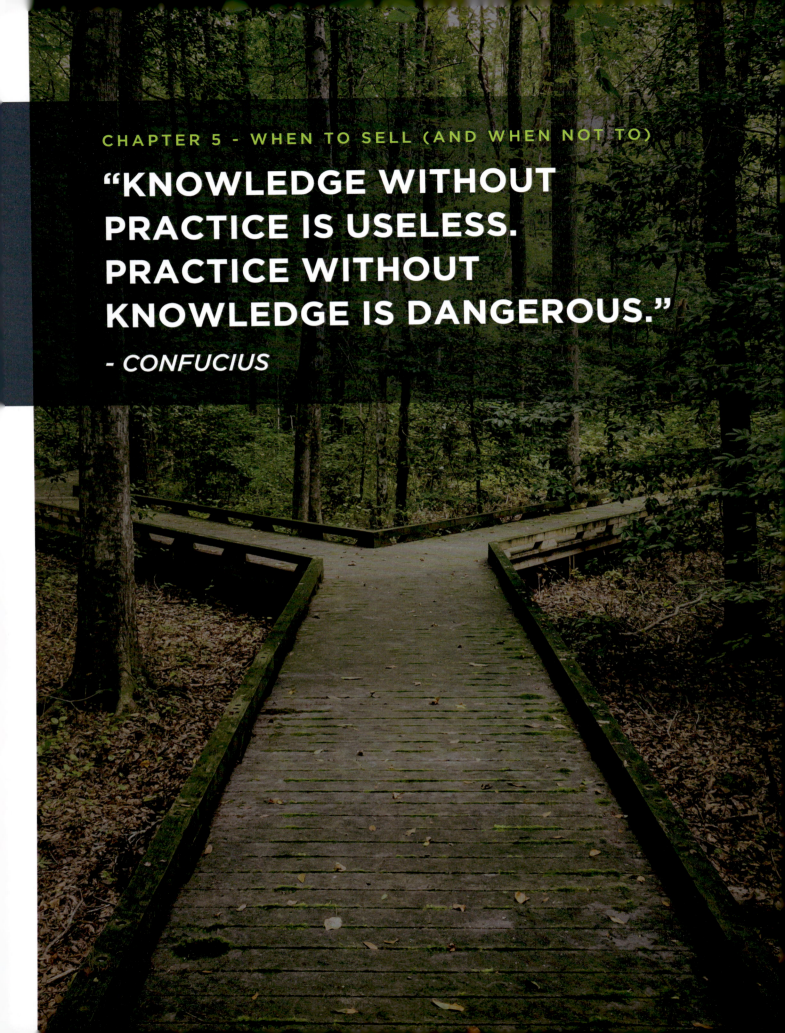

CHAPTER 5 - WHEN TO SELL (AND WHEN NOT TO)

"KNOWLEDGE WITHOUT PRACTICE IS USELESS. PRACTICE WITHOUT KNOWLEDGE IS DANGEROUS."

- CONFUCIUS

■ FINISH STRONG

As I said in the book... Imagine if you hold on just 3% too long in your overall business journey. Twelve extra months in 30 years of ownership is no big deal, right? Unfortunately, as the graph shows, it can be a very big deal. That 3% in extra time could cost you 20-40% or more in value if you are burned out and business performance is declining.

Many sellers are mentally exhausted before they even give us a call. Still, we urge them to push strong for one more year. Make the last year the best. If sales and profits are increasing because you are sprinting to that finish line, your business will be more salable.

The best time to sell is when you don't have to. *Sprint to the end.*

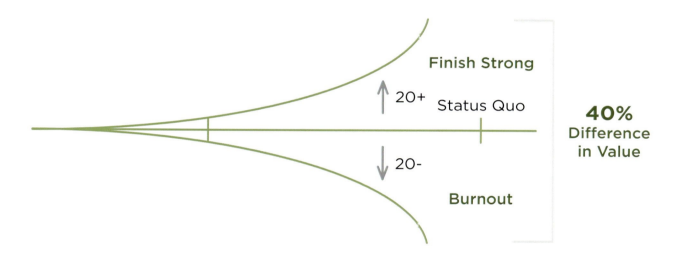

■ BUILD YOUR DREAM TEAM

Always work with specialists. You might have the best relationship in the world with your general practitioner, but if you need angioplasty, you go to a heart surgeon. Same goes for business. Your M&A attorney and M&A advisor should be specialists. Even if you are years from going to market, these advisors will be able to share current M&A market trends and give you insight to enhance value and make your company more salable.

CPA

Company Name	Contact Name
Office Number	Cell Number
Email	

Attorney

Company Name	Contact Name
Office Number	Cell Number
Email	

M&A Attorney

Company Name	Contact Name
Office Number	Cell Number
Email	

Financial Advisor

Company Name	Contact Name
Office Number	Cell Number
Email	

M&A Advisor

Company Name	Contact Name
Office Number	Cell Number
Email	

Exit Planner/Value Enhancement Consultant

Company Name	Contact Name
Office Number	Cell Number
Email	

PLEASE DO NOT SKIP THIS EXERCISE!

■ THE THREE LEGGED STOOL

Knowledge = power. Think of an exit plan like a three-legged stool. Your exit strategy is supported by information and guidance from an investment banker, a CPA, and a financial advisor.

Total Number: Get an estimate of value (EOV). An investment banker/M&A advisor will help you understand your business' realistic value in today's M&A marketplace.

Net Number: Once you know what your business is worth, ask your CPA to do a tax analysis and determine what you'd net after a sale. Find out what tax-planning strategies—if any—you should be implementing now.

Lifestyle Number™: Meet with your financial advisor and determine if your business value and after-tax proceeds will support your ideal retirement and legacy goals.

Total Number _____ - Debt/taxes _____ = Net Number

Net Number _____ ≥ Lifestyle Number™ _____ = Sell

Net Number _____ < Lifestyle Number™ _____ =
1. Lower or rejust Lifestyle Number™ to equal Net Number
2. Value enhancement — go back to step one in the Assurance 360 process

_____ Total Number
_____ Net Number
_____ Lifestyle Number™

Owner trying to do on their own - Unstable *With the help of specialists - Strong foundation*

■ TOTAL COMPENSATION

This exercise will help you better understand exactly what you are taking out of the company. These are the most common ways we see owners derive value from the business. This will allow you to make sure you are not under or over stating what your current income stream is for future planning.

	HISTORICAL OR PAST		
	Year 2	Year 1	TTM
Salary			
Bonus			
Health benefits: what dollar amount paid by company			
Life insurance: premiums paid by company			
Personal expenses: vacations, country club, family members on payroll who don't work for the business			
Auto expense: any personal auto expense for family members, purchase of vehicle, fuel, insurance, maintenance			
401K/benefits			
Other			
Distribution: money from the profits of the business. This will affect the balance sheet, not the P&L.			
TOTAL			
One time costs: What are any one-time costs incurred in any year, above and beyond normal ongoing year-to-year expenses?			
TOTAL			
Salary adjustments: If you were to hire a person to fill your current role, what would it cost in salary, benefits, etc. How does this compare to your current salary?			
Rent adjustments: If you own the real estate in a separate entity, or personally, what would be the fair market rent if you were to lease it to a 3rd party? How does that compare with the current rent you are paying yourself?			

CHAPTER 6 - HOW TO AVOID SELLER'S REMORSE

"JUST BECAUSE YOUR LIFE CHANGES DOESN'T MEAN THAT YOUR DEEPEST PASSIONS HAVE TO." - SHANNON MILLER

■ YOUR BUCKET LIST

As you're thinking about exiting your business, it's time to plan your own bucket list. Because if you don't spend time looking ahead, you'll let fear of the unknown get in the way of a sale.

What have you always wanted to do, but owning the business made it impossible? What promises have you made to others close to you that are still unfulfilled? Where can you transfer that energy and passion? There are no "wrong answers." What do you want to do or be in your next best chapter?

1
2
3
4
5
6
7
8
9
10

■ REMEMBER ME

At the end of the day, when you reflect on your life, what do you want to be known for?

■ YOUR PASSIONS
What do you love? What are you willing to fight for? What fills you with energy or delight?

family   volunteering   gardening

traveling   kids

woodworking   biking   painting

new business   grandkids

■ HOW DO YOU WANT TO MAKE THE WORLD A BETTER PLACE?
What would you like to support with time or money?

■ **WHAT ARE THE THREE THINGS THAT HOLD YOU BACK FROM LIVING YOUR BEST LIFE?**

1

2

3

"THE TWO MOST IMPORTANT DAYS IN YOUR LIFE ARE THE DAY YOU ARE BORN AND THE DAY YOU FIND OUT WHY."
- MARK TWAIN.

CHAPTER 7 - NOT ALL BUYERS ARE CREATED EQUAL

"BEAUTY LIES IN THE EYES OF THE BEHOLDER"

▪ VALUE IS A FUNCTION OF RISK VS REWARD

Valuation is based on risk, real or perceived, and future cash flows for the buyer. What will actually transfer to the new buyer? The more you enhance your business and take away a buyer's pain points, the more attractive your company will be, the more offers you will receive, and the greater the value you will realize.

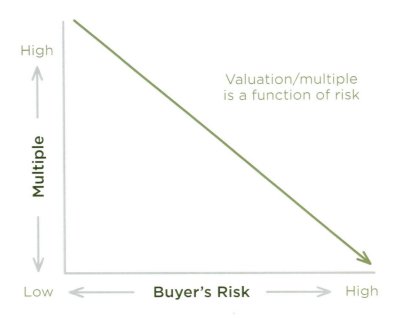

▪ REVENUE AND TTM CHARTS

Chart revenue and EBITDA for the last three years, the trailing 12 months (TTM), and future projections. In the TTM tables, chart the last 12 months – then continue to add new months to see your trend line. Buyers ideally want a business trending up, and they place the most value on TTM and future cash flow.

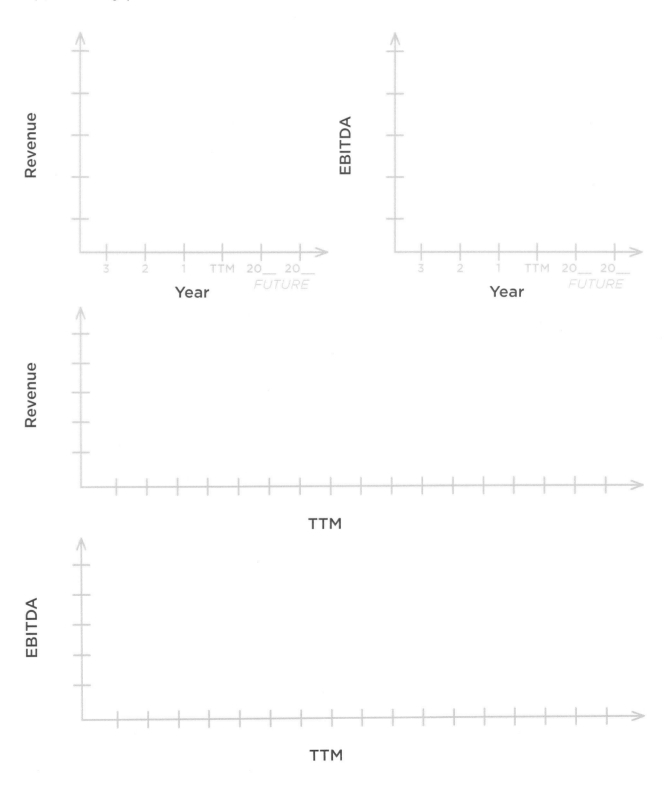

■ BUSINESS VALUE CHARACTERISTICS

Here's a high-level snapshot of the drivers that can influence your business value. Each industry is unique so some categories may not be as applicable to you. Give us a call. We would be happy to share our insight on your particular business and industry.

CUSTOMERS

BELOW INDUSTRY AVERAGE	INDUSTRY AVERAGE	ABOVE INDUSTRY AVERAGE
• Top 3 customers > 90% of revenue • MSA with PO's • Local mom/pops are only customers • Owner takes all the phone calls from customer	• Top 10 customers < 50% of revenue • Annual contracts • Middle market/regional businesses • Dedicated salesman on the team • Mix of one-time/recurring revenue	• No customer more than 5% of revenue • Multi-year contracts • Blue chip multinationals • Full sales team that manage customers • Small, recurring purchases

INDUSTRY AND END MARKETS

BELOW INDUSTRY AVERAGE	INDUSTRY AVERAGE	ABOVE INDUSTRY AVERAGE
• Completely discretionary • Small market size that is shrinking • Boom or bust • Heavy government pressures/regulation that constrain the business	• Should / need to have your solution • Low market growth • Cyclical business; correlated to GDP • Heavy government pressures/regulation that promote the business	• Product/service is "non discretionary" • Large market; growing rapidly • Steady business; grew through the recession • Little government involvement

SUPPLIERS

BELOW INDUSTRY AVERAGE	INDUSTRY AVERAGE	ABOVE INDUSTRY AVERAGE
• Top 3 suppliers > 90% of revenue • No contracts • Core operations outsourced to supplier • Suppliers can sell directly to your customer base	• Top 10 supplier < 50% of revenue • Annual contracts • Painful to switch suppliers, but not a death blow • Occasional/hybrid competition	• No supplier more than 5% of revenue • Multi-year supply agreements with exclusivity • Easy to bring in new suppliers • Exclusivity/non-compete as part of contract

COMPETITION

BELOW INDUSTRY AVERAGE	INDUSTRY AVERAGE	ABOVE INDUSTRY AVERAGE
• High commodity products with low margins • Thousands of competitors; no differentiation • Easy for new competitors to emerge and copy what you are doing	• Limited alternatives to your products with average margins • Balanced market share across the industry • New entrants would require significant investment to compete	• Proprietary products with high margins • Market leader with few competitors • Significant capabilities that would be hard to recreate

MANAGEMENT & FINANCIALS

BELOW INDUSTRY AVERAGE	INDUSTRY AVERAGE	ABOVE INDUSTRY AVERAGE
• Little to no accounting systems • No CPA involvement • One man operation or no management team depth • No professional accounting staff	• Limited information systems • Compiled or reviewed financials • One or two person senior management team • Controller on staff	• Sophisticated information systems • Audited financials • Well-rounded management team • Full-time CPA/CFO on staff

■ WORKING CAPITAL PEG

A/R (Accounts Receivables) + Inv (Inventory) – A/P (Accounts Payable) = WC Peg. Most times the established WC Peg is the average TTM needs of the company for WC.

Sometimes, prepaids are added to the current assets, while accruals are added to current liabilities. Items typically excluded are cash (unless tied to customer deposits/advancements), notes to and from the owner or related party (i.e., Notes Receivable or Notes Payable), long-term debt, and most times, the Line of Credit.

Most owners have not tracked or analyzed their working capital before. Your accountant should be able to assist you — if not we can help.
This is a big deal in most sales.

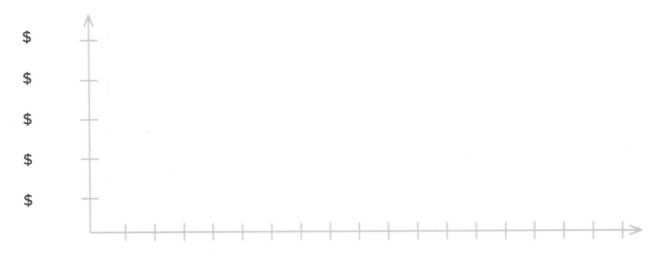

TTM

It's important to understand your average working capital peg for the 2 calendar years prior. This allows you to compare where the TTM trend is going vs where it was in past years.

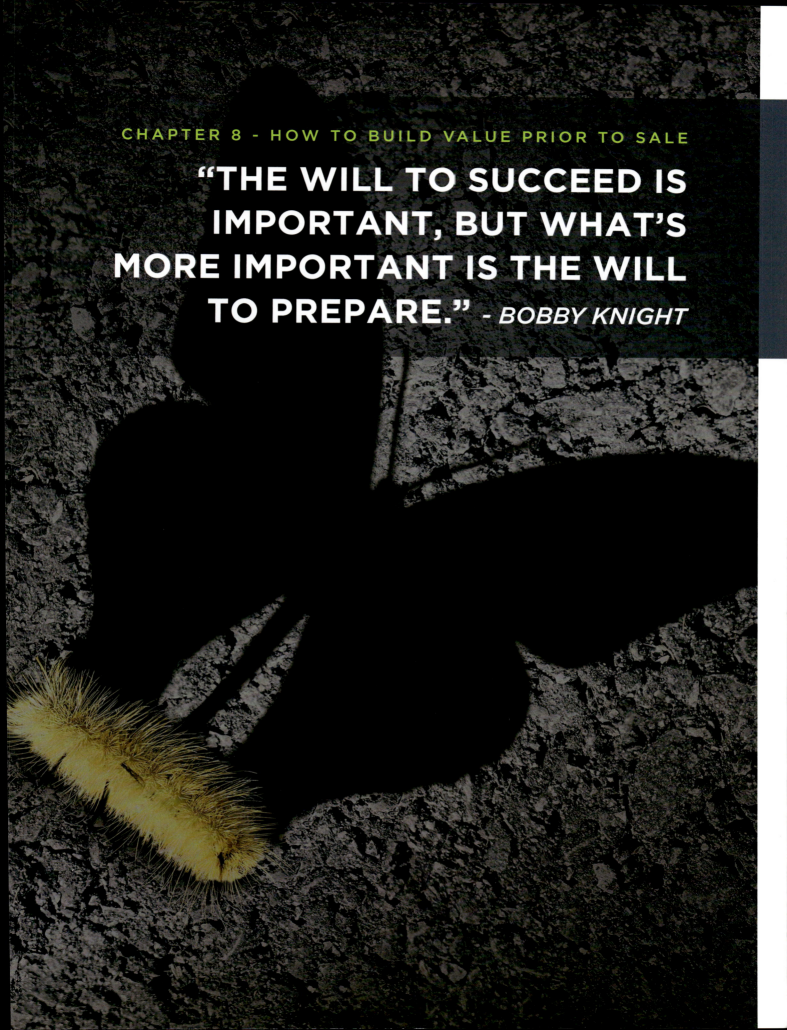

CHAPTER 8 - HOW TO BUILD VALUE PRIOR TO SALE

"THE WILL TO SUCCEED IS IMPORTANT, BUT WHAT'S MORE IMPORTANT IS THE WILL TO PREPARE." - *BOBBY KNIGHT*

■ SWOT

The SWOT is a classic business analysis tool. Think about how your company will most likely succeed and where it could possibly fail.

STRENGTHS
What are the internal capabilities, attributes, skills and/or assets within your control that set you apart from the competition? Strengths define your competitive advantage.

1
2
3
4
5

OPPORTUNITIES
What trends and opportunities currently exist in the industry, marketplace, community, and/or the world that could help the organization grow faster, be more profitable, and/or become more valuable?

1
2
3
4
5

WEAKNESSES
What are the internal factors within your control that limit your competitiveness or detract from your value? What does the organization not do very well that we should work to eliminate?

1
2
3
4
5

THREATS
What threats exist externally beyond your control that could really hurt the ability of the organization to operate and/or be profitable? Threats can't be eliminated, but steps can be taken to mitigate their impact.

1
2
3
4
5

"SUCCESS IS WHERE PREPARATION AND OPPORTUNITY MEET."
- BOBBY UNSER

■ TWELVE MONTH VACATION CALENDAR

This exercise is a fun one. But it's also one that's necessary to stretch your team. Map out some vacation time. I recommend noting key birthdays or anniversaries, too. The goal is to build up to at least four one-week vacations. Better yet, can you take two weeks off with little to no interruptions? One of the top value drivers is a strong management team, and this is a way to test yours over a period of time.

January
Week 1
Week 2
Week 3
Week 4

February
Week 1
Week 2
Week 3
Week 4

March
Week 1
Week 2
Week 3
Week 4

April
Week 1
Week 2
Week 3
Week 4

May
Week 1
Week 2
Week 3
Week 4

June
Week 1
Week 2
Week 3
Week 4

July
Week 1
Week 2
Week 3
Week 4

August
Week 1
Week 2
Week 3
Week 4

September
Week 1
Week 2
Week 3
Week 4

October
Week 1
Week 2
Week 3
Week 4

November
Week 1
Week 2
Week 3
Week 4

December
Week 1
Week 2
Week 3
Week 4

■ REVIEW AND COMPLETE THE VALUE DRIVERS CHECKLIST

Initial each box when it is completed or at least contemplated. Depending on the type and size of your business, not all items may apply. But the vast majority, if implemented, should help make your company more valuable and salable. (Items in green reflect those items buyers tend to care about most.)

☐ **1. Drive cash to bottom line**
- Ideally for the last three years prior to sale, eliminate personal expenses. Even if only for one year, it will help you get a better value. Remember: Cash is King!

☐ **2. Complete the working capital exercise**
- Focus on driving down A/R and inventory. Extend your A/P as long as you can without damaging any relationships. Carefully reducing your working capital will put more money in your pocket at the time of sale—in many cases hundreds of thousands of dollars! Your CPA should be able to help you here if you have questions.

☐ **3. Stay bonus**
- Consider whether you should offer stay bonuses to key management or employees when you go to market. Typically, you might extend bonuses to employees you need to bring into the sales process to sell the company and/or the ones running your business. Think of this as an insurance policy to help sell your company and maximize value. It is also a nice "thank you" to those who helped you build the company.

- Your advisor will help you determine when to offer a bonus and how much. I have seen everything from 50% of salary to $500K. In my experience, many are around 1x annual salary or some amount that is large enough to get their attention. I have seen the most success when owners give 50% at close and the balance 6-12 months later.

- Do not draft this yourself. Have an experienced attorney draft it for you—preferably an M&A specialist.

☐ **4. Non-compete agreements**
- All management and key employees should have signed one of these to help protect your business. They should also be assignable to a new owner.

- If agreements are already in place, review with an attorney and confirm the agreements are current, transferable, and enforceable as the laws in each state are different and continue to change. Again, have an experienced attorney review/draft these for you.

5. Document processes:

• Get all ideas, processes, quoting and any other proprietary steps of "how you do business" down on paper or better yet digitally into a program your employees can access and use. This helps create consistency and reduces the risk of one person "being the business."

6. Do you have any contracts? Customer? Supplier?

• Are the contracts assignable or do you need approval from another party? Is there a way to get the contracts assignable before you go to market? Make sure an attorney reviews the contracts to confirm.

7. Spring cleaning

• Have you taken the time to organize and clean both the exterior and interior of your facility? Does it look like you take pride in your facility/office? Buyers will notice.

• Is your own office organized and clean? Buyers may assume that what they see in your office reflects how the company is managed. Does your office scream order or chaos?

8. Audit for past 3 years or a Quality of Earnings (QofE) report prior to going to market

• We typically recommend this for companies with $10M or more in revenue, but it is a great investment for smaller companies as well. I have been told by multiple buyers that they will pay more for a company that has one of the above completed by a reputable CPA firm prior to going to market.

Longer term value add items

9. Develop the management team

• You want to work your way out of the business. The less valuable you are to the company's day to day operations and sales, the more valuable the company is to another buyer.

• How can you invest in your team? Virtual education, conferences, workshops, certification courses? Owners routinely invest in equipment or physical assets; don't forget about the human assets.

• Consider how you can mentor your team prior to a sale.

• Work to transition all customer relationships to one or more of your employees.

Continued on next page.

VALUE DRIVERS CHECKLIST CONTINUED...

10. Increase your sales/profit trends

• What is the trajectory of your business? Buyers will typically pay much more for one on the increase vs. the decline. Work to finish strong.

11. Diversification

• Buyers are most concerned about customer diversification, but supplier diversification can be an issue too. No one customer should be more than 20%-25% of annual sales.

• How can you diversify your customer base? How can you find new customers or sell more to existing customers to eliminate the dependence on one large account?

• Do you have duplicate sources for all the products or services supplied to your business? If you only have one supplier for a mission critical piece of your business, it will lower the value. Remember the higher the risk the lower the multiple.

▌ TOP CUSTOMER LIST

Review your top customers. If you depend on one large customer for a significant portion of sales, talk to us about how that could impact your exit strategy.

	CUSTOMER	% OF SALES
1		
2		
3		
4		
5		

■ 168 HOURS

We all get 168 hours a week. Once we spend those hours, we can't get them back. Consider how much time you're working "in" the business (day to day obligations) and how much time you're working "on" the business (coaching, strategy, development).

And, think about how much time you're working versus the hours a new owner or employed executive would reasonably put in. When you cut back on your hours and/or shift your time to working "on" the business, you show a buyer that the company can function without your constant oversight.

Example

ACTIVITY	HOURS DAILY	DAYS PER WEEK	HOURS WEEKLY
SLEEPING	7.5	7	52.5
EATING	1.5	7	10.5
WORKING "IN" BUSINESS	8	6	48
WORKING "ON" BUSINESS	1	5	5
SELF-CARE	.1	7	7
Exercise	1	7	7
HOURS SPOKEN FOR EACH WEEK			130
TIME LEFT OVER EACH WEEK			38

Are you spending your work time the way you want?
Are you satisfied with the extra time you have for yourself and your family?

Chart how you'd like to be spending your time:

ACTIVITY	HOURS DAILY	DAYS PER WEEK	HOURS WEEKLY
SLEEPING			
EATING			
WORKING "IN" BUSINESS			
WORKING "ON" BUSINESS			
SELF-CARE			
HOURS SPOKEN FOR EACH WEEK			
TIME LEFT OVER EACH WEEK			

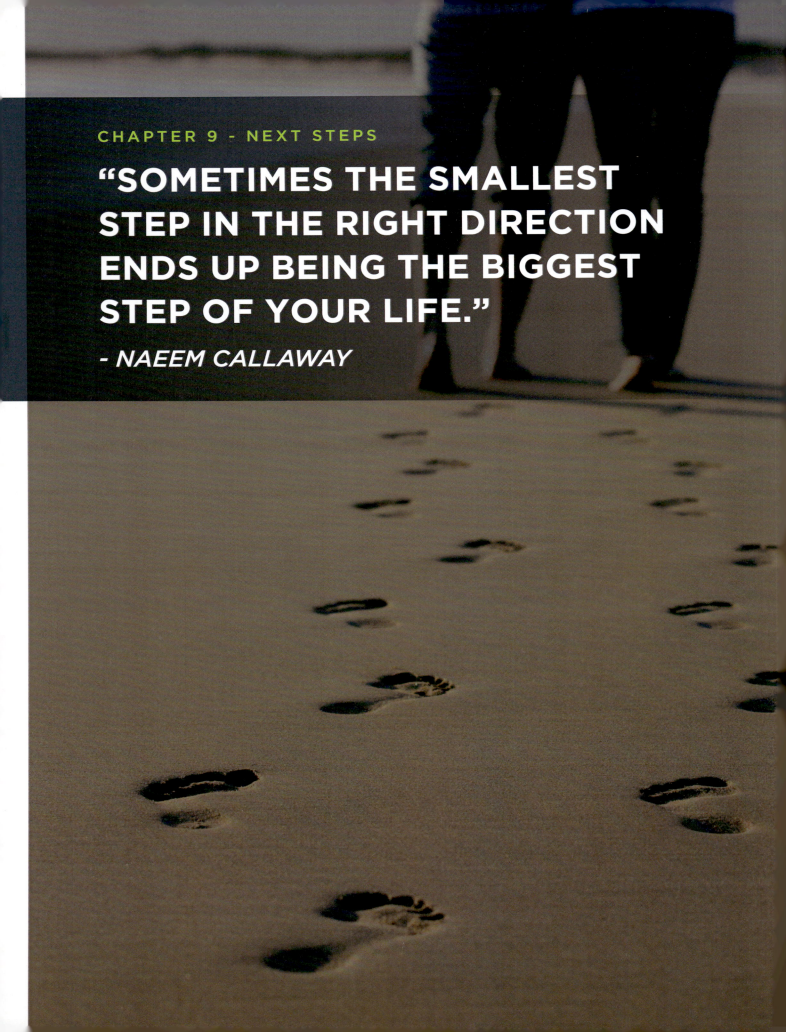

CHAPTER 9 - NEXT STEPS

"SOMETIMES THE SMALLEST STEP IN THE RIGHT DIRECTION ENDS UP BEING THE BIGGEST STEP OF YOUR LIFE."

— NAEEM CALLAWAY

▪ LET'S RECAP

Let's get a snapshot of where you're at. Take some of the key numbers you filled out earlier in the book and transfer them here.

Sales *(See Chapter 5)*   **EBITDA** *(See Chapter 5)*

PAST
20__
20__
20__
TTM

FUTURE
20__
20__

Known Exit Window
(Time-frame/age to be out)

Top Two Preferred Exit Options 1. _____   2. _____

Total Number _____   Net Number _____   Lifestyle Number™ _____

Is the Net Number ≥ Lifestyle Number™   Yes/No

Now is the time to implement the ideas in Finish Strong: Selling Your Business on Your Terms and in this workbook. An exit strategy protects the value of the business you've built, protects your family, and protects your legacy.

■ YOUR NEXT STEPS

- [ ] CALL FOR A MARKET UPDATE. WE'LL HAVE A CONFIDENTIAL, NO-COST DISCUSSION TO EDUCATE YOU ON CURRENT MARKET CONDITIONS AND HELP ANSWER OTHER QUESTIONS YOU HAVE.

- [ ] GET AN ESTIMATE OF VALUE. FIND OUT HOW MUCH YOUR COMPANY IS WORTH SO YOU CAN UNDERSTAND YOUR TOTAL NUMBER.

  - [ ] • MEET WITH YOUR CPA TO UNDERSTAND YOUR NET NUMBER.

  - [ ] • MEET WITH YOUR FINANCIAL ADVISOR TO UNDERSTAND YOUR ALL IMPORTANT LIFESTYLE NUMBER™.

- [ ] IF YOU'RE NOT READY TO SELL AND KNOW YOU NEED TO ENHANCE VALUE, WE CAN GIVE YOU A LIST OF TRUSTED CONSULTANTS WHO CAN HELP YOU EXPEDITE THAT PROCESS.

- [ ] START PREPARING TODAY. DON'T PROCRASTINATE.
  If you have any questions whatsoever, please don't hesitate to call Cornerstone Business Services at 920-436-9890 or email sbushkie@cornerstone-business.com.

- [ ] GET EXCITED ABOUT YOUR FUTURE. YOUR BEST CHAPTER IS STILL AHEAD.

**HONEST CONVERSATIONS
SUPERIOR RESULTS**

Valuing, Buying, and Selling BUSINESSES NATIONWIDE SINCE 2001
It's our mission to create positive life-changing events for all the lives we touch.

920-436-9890 | WWW.CORNERSTONE-BUSINESS.COM

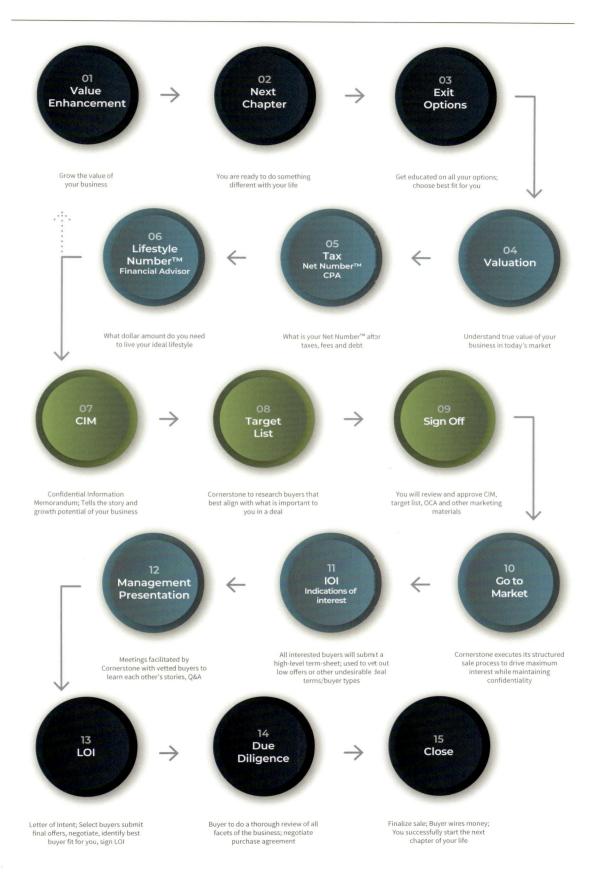

■ SMART GOALS

Now's the time to define your next steps. You've probably heard of SMART goals before – they're Specific, Measurable, Achievable, Relevant, and Time-bound. Hold yourself accountable to action by keeping this list somewhere you'll see it every day.

Goal Deadline _____

My Specific Goal is...
_____
_____
_____
_____

I Know I Will Reach My Goal When...
_____
_____
_____

I Know I Can Reach this Goal Because...
_____
_____
_____

My Personal Values Tied to this Goal Are...
_____
_____
_____

Goal Deadline _____

My Specific Goal is...
_____
_____
_____
_____

I Know I Will Reach My Goal When...
_____
_____
_____

I Know I Can Reach this Goal Because...
_____
_____
_____

My Personal Values Tied to this Goal Are...
_____
_____
_____